Play in the Wild

For Dave
With special thanks to Connie, Megan, and Monique

Copyright © 2020 by Lita Judge
Published by Roaring Brook Press
Roaring Brook Press is a division of Holtzbrinck Publishing Holdings Limited Partnership
120 Broadway, New York, NY 10271
mackids.com

Library of Congress Cataloging-in-Publication Data

Names: Judge, Lita, author.
Title: Play in the wild: how baby animals like to have fun / Lita Judge.
Description: First edition. | New York : Roaring Brook Press, 2020. |
Series: In the wild; 3 | Audience: Ages 5–8 | Audience: Grades K–1 |
Summary: "An adorable nonfiction picture book by Lita Judge about the
many ways baby animals engage in play and how play helps them grow"—Provided by publisher.
Identifiers: LCCN 20190442169 | ISBN 9781250237064 (hardcover)
Subjects: LCSH: Play behavior in animals—Juvenile literature. |
Animals—Infancy—Juvenile literature.
Classification: LCC QL763.5.J83 2020 | DDC 591.3/92—dc23
LC record available at https://lccn.loc.gov/2019042169

ISBN: 978-1-250-23706-4

Our books may be purchased in bulk for promotional, educational, or business use. Please contact your local
bookseller or the Macmillan Corporate and Premium Sales Department at (800) 221-7945 ext. 5442 or
by email at MacmillanSpecialMarkets@macmillan.com.

First edition, 2020
Book design by Monique Sterling
Printed in China by RR Donnelley Asia Printing Solutions Ltd., Dongguan City, Guangdong Province

1 3 5 7 9 10 8 6 4 2

Play in the Wild

How Baby Animals Like to Have Fun

Lita Judge

ROARING BROOK PRESS

New York

Pounce, leap, chase, and slide,

young animals like to play.

Red river hog piglets butt heads in frisky shoving matches, run in circles, and turn found objects into toys by tossing them up in the air.

A pair of **red panda** cubs bat each other with their paws and jump, tackle, and roll around for some rough-and-tumble fun.

There is still much we don't know about the animal world, but through careful observation, scientists are discovering how animals play and why.

Many young animals
ask first before playing.

"Attack" games can be mistaken for picking a fight, so before they charge and tackle, some young animals use a special signal to invite a sibling or friend to play.

A young **chimpanzee** swings his head and shoulders from side to side (called gamboling) while smiling and bouncing. That is his way of asking his friend, "Do you want to play with me?" If she looks interested, he might hit her lightly on the shoulder and run away. That means "The game is on!"

When **sea lions** are swimming, they can't use their body posture to show they want to play. Instead, one pup approaches another while holding a piece of kelp that serves as a toy, then quickly swims away, as if to announce, "Chase me!"

A **yellow mongoose** pup whistles to his littermates to invite them to wrestle. The pups continue to whistle as they pounce and gently bite each other, as opposed to growling, which means "This fight is real," or screaming, which means "That hurts!"

Play helps young animals learn to find food.

Through play, some young animals discover
where to forage for food or how to catch it.

Arctic fox pups jump, jump, jump, as if their legs were springs, when they hear the
faintest sound of a lemming running beneath the snow. Catching prey they can't see isn't easy, but
someday they will be able to judge where to punch through the crusty ice for a much-needed meal.

Young **capuchin monkeys** are curious about everything. Using objects as toys during creative play helps them develop thinking and problem-solving skills. Some capuchins even learn how to use rocks as tools to break open hard nuts.

Cheetah cubs crouch and stalk each other, then pounce, swat, and bite. Their games are not just fun; they are also important for mastering hunting skills. Cubs who play more become better at catching live prey.

Even during play,
young animals follow
the rules.

No one wants to get hurt while playing, even when roughhousing, so animals have to play fair.

While scuffling, young **rats** make a chirping sound, much like the way humans laugh (though it is too high-pitched for our ears to hear). During their playful matches, they tickle each other's necks with their snouts. They never raise their fur to appear large and aggressive, or bite hard, as they do when they are really fighting.

Yellow-bellied marmot pups and yearlings stand on their hind legs to play-box, nose-push, and knock each other over. Later, matches between males will be real and fierce to determine dominance. But for now, no growling or biting!

Even grown-ups like to play. When a male **lion** tussles with his high-spirited cub, he may pin her in a headlock with his huge mouth. But he only pretends to bite. Around him, his litter of cubs pounces and attacks! They swat lightly and keep their claws retracted so they don't scratch him.

Play can build

communities.

Through play, young animals who live in tight communities learn how to get along.

Young **rhesus monkeys** play a lot of contact sports like slapping and brawling. They also love a round of hide-and-seek. While playing, they learn how to read each other's expressions, an important skill for living within a tight-knit social group.

Baby **elephants** are too bulky to tussle with their bodies. Instead they grapple with their trunks, entwining them, and poke each other all over. If water is nearby, watch out: A trunk makes a perfect spray hose! This physical contact builds connections between them that last a lifetime.

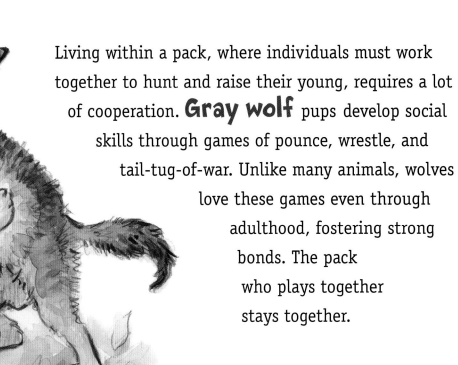

Living within a pack, where individuals must work together to hunt and raise their young, requires a lot of cooperation. **Gray wolf** pups develop social skills through games of pounce, wrestle, and tail-tug-of-war. Unlike many animals, wolves love these games even through adulthood, fostering strong bonds. The pack who plays together stays together.

Play can be practice

for finding a mate.

Male animals often have to compete with one another to breed. The competition can be fierce, so many young animals develop important skills through play-fighting.

Polar bear cubs stand on their hind legs and battle in mock fights. For now, they aren't trying to hurt each other with their sharp teeth and claws, but someday the males will fight for real, ferociously competing for a mate.

Nubian ibex kids spring vertically in the air, jump on each other, and knock heads. These rounds of "King of the Mountain" may prepare male billies for the challenges they face in adulthood. Adult male ibexes compete for a mate by crashing their long horns into each other like battering rams.

Red-necked wallaby joeys hop, kick, and push each other with their front paws. If mother joins the fun, she stands flat-footed, so her powerful legs won't harm her small joey. When the males grow to adulthood, their boxing matches will turn serious. Wallabies determine dominance and compete for a mate through forceful kicking and shoving matches.

Sometimes when playing,

It's natural for excitement to take over. When young animals accidentally hurt or scare their playmates, they apologize.

A **colobus monkey** initiates a good game of tag by slapping her friend's leg lightly, or even shaking a stick at him. But if she gets too rough, her playmate will back away. After a time-out, the monkey may try a friendly bouncing walk or a gentler slap to see if her friend has forgiven her. She may even let her partner chase her instead.

While mock sparring, a **golden jackal** kit gets carried away and aggressively bites her sibling. He stops playing and moves away. When she approaches him again, she wags her tail in a friendly way and playfully bows to say "I didn't mean to be so rough." Usually her sibling will trust her apology and will bark and bow in response. Then, the play will start again.

In the heat of play battle, a young **gorilla** bites his playmate too hard. His bitten friend then stops playing. She squints her eyes and tilts her head as if to say "That hurt!" To show he is sorry, he puts a hand on her shoulder. He may even groom her until she feels safe and forgives—and then they can resume their game.

Play can mean survival.

For many young animals, energetic play increases their chances of growing into adulthood.

Feral horse colts frolic, kick up their heels, and chase one another. Their constant game looks like a lot of fun, but their romping has a serious side. Colts who run and leap a lot grow faster and are less likely to become a predator's dinner.

Brown bear cubs are naturally curious and see everything they find as potential for making a game. Whether bouncing at the end of a tree limb, ripping apart an old log, or playing a game of tug-of-war with a piece of elk hide, their creative play builds coordination and teaches them to find future food sources.

Belding's ground squirrel pups cuff each other and tumble in mock fistfights. Scientists have observed that friskier pups grow stronger and are more likely to become healthier adults than less playful pups. Spirited female pups have a greater chance later of raising pups to adulthood.

Play can be for fun.

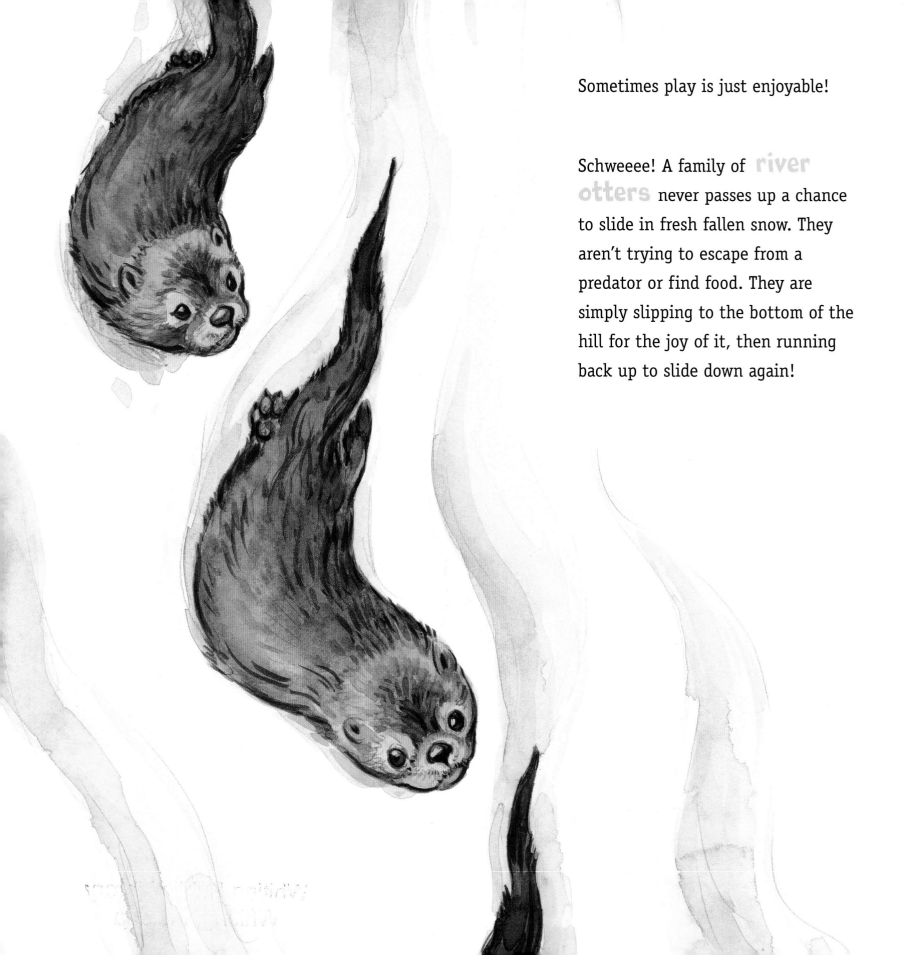

Sometimes play is just enjoyable!

Schweeee! A family of river otters never passes up a chance to slide in fresh fallen snow. They aren't trying to escape from a predator or find food. They are simply slipping to the bottom of the hill for the joy of it, then running back up to slide down again!

A **raven** swoops and circles low over a **coyote's** head, teasing him into a game of chase. The coyote runs and jumps after him. Sometimes the raven pauses on the ground, waiting for his friend to catch up. Neither is hunting; they are only loving a game of "Catch Me If You Can" on a bright day.

A **bottlenose dolphin** creates a toy by blowing bubbles through the blowhole at the top of her head. Then, by tossing her head into the vortices, she turns the bubbles into a silvery ring. She even shares it with a friend as they both chase the ring with their noses.

Cubs and kits, joeys and kittens—
young animals like to play . . .

just like you!

More about the animals in this book

Red river hogs inhabit rivers and swamps of Central Africa. They live in small groups composed of a single adult male, several adult females, and their young. Mothers give birth to an average of two to six piglets. Both mother and father help care for and protect young. They eat roots, nuts, tubers, fruit, grasses, eggs, insects, lizards, and carrion. Hogs use their large muzzles and tusks to snuffle and scrape about in the soil in search of food.

Red pandas are solitary animals living in the forested, mountainous regions of the eastern Himalayas and southwestern China. They spend most of their time in trees to escape jackals and leopards and to find food. Bamboo makes up to ninety-five percent of their diet. Mothers give birth to one to four cubs, raising them alone. The cubs stay with their mother until the next litter is born in the following summer. Adults are roughly the size of a domestic cat, though with longer bodies.

Common chimpanzees are social and live in groups known as communities. Females bear only one baby at a time. Newborns are helpless and cling to the fur of the mother's belly for the first two months. They are dependent on their mother's milk for up to six years. Chimps communicate with facial expressions, gestures, and a large array of vocalizations. Their "play panting" and grinning look similar to human laughter and smiling. Chimpanzees live in a variety of habitats, including the dry savanna, rain forests, and woodlands of Equatorial Africa. They prefer fruit but will also eat leaves, seeds, blossoms, bark, insects, and carrion.

California sea lions are native to the western coast of North America. They dive up to twelve hundred feet deep in search of fish, octopus, and squid to eat. They can also swim about eighteen miles per hour for short bursts when escaping killer whales and sharks. The females give birth to a single pup and remain onshore for ten days to nurse them. After this, mothers leave for up to three days at a time to hunt. Pups left onshore gather in nurseries to socialize and play.

Yellow mongooses are very social, living in colonies of up to twenty individuals. They may share their underground burrows with ground squirrels or meerkats. If threatened, they growl and screech to warn one another or to scare off a predator. They bark when they want to play. Mothers have litters of two to five pups who play nearly constantly. Mongooses feed mainly on insects and other invertebrates but also hunt amphibians, rodents, and reptiles. They live in the semi-desert scrubland and grasslands of Southern Africa.

Cheetahs are the fastest land animal, running up to fifty-eight miles per hour for short bursts while hunting. Adult females are solitary, but males remain together in groups of two to three called a "coalition." A mother raises her litter of three to five cubs on her own. When they are about six months old, she will bring live prey for them to practice hunting. They inhabit the dry forests and savannas of Southern, North, and East Africa, and Iran.

The Arctic fox lives in some of the most frigid extremes on the planet, throughout the Arctic of the Northern Hemisphere. Incredibly hardy, they can survive temperatures as low as fifty-eight degrees below zero. The color of their coat changes with the seasons, turning from white when the tundra is snow-covered to dark in the summer. Their birth rate is linked closely to the population of their main prey, lemmings. When lemmings are abundant, an Arctic fox can give birth to up to eighteen pups but will have no pups when food is scarce. Arctic foxes mate for life, and both mother and father raise their pups together.

The tufted capuchin is a primate from South America, living mainly in the Amazon basin. They feed mainly on fruits and invertebrates but will sometimes consume small lizards, bird chicks, and plant material. Unlike most animals, they have been observed making tools to forage. They have been known to use containers to hold water, sticks to dig, sponges to absorb juice, and stones as hammer and anvil to crack nuts. They are social, forming groups of eight to fifteen individuals that are led by a dominant male.

Alongside humans, the brown rat is the most successful mammal on the planet, spreading to all continents except Antarctica. These rodents breed throughout the year, and females can have up to five litters a year, with six to eleven pups in each litter. They are good swimmers, and in the wild, they prefer damp environments, such as riverbanks. There they eat grain, insects, snails, fish and mussels, small birds, mammals, and reptiles. But they are also highly adaptable to living within towns and cities, scavenging through trash.

Yellow-bellied marmots are native to the mountainous regions of southwestern Canada and western United States. Because of the long winters of their high-altitude range, they hibernate about eight months of the year. They live in communal burrows, feeding on plants, insects, and bird eggs. Females within a group have three to eight pups. Members of the same colony play together and groom one another. They communicate through whistles, screams, and tooth chatter, as well as body language.

The lion is the most social of all wild cat species, living in groups of up to forty individuals, called "prides." These groups consist of related females, their cubs, yearlings, and one or more males. The female lions raise the cubs and are also the primary hunters. Males defend the pride from attacking predators. Each female typically gives birth to a litter of one to four cubs every two years. Lions primarily hunt large animals such as zebra and wildebeest, but they will also steal kills from hyenas, leopards, and other predators. They inhabit the grasslands and savannas of Africa and India.

The gray wolf, also known as timber wolf, is native to the remote wilderness of Eurasia and North America. They are social animals, living in packs composed of a mated pair, their adult offspring, and an average litter of five to six pups. Mated pairs usually remain together for life. The pack works together to hunt large prey, such as deer and moose. Wolves also eat smaller mammals and fruit. Pups begin play-fighting at the age of three weeks.

Native to South, Central, and Southeast Asia, rhesus macaques inhabit a wide range of habitats, from grasslands, woodlands, and mountainous regions, while also living close to human settlements. They climb easily but spend much of their time on the ground. They are also good swimmers. They live in large groups, consisting of twenty to two hundred males and females, called "troops," interacting with one another by using facial expressions, vocalizations, and body postures. Females usually have one baby each year. Rhesus macaques feed mainly on fruit but also eat other plant material.

The **African bush elephant** is the largest land animal, with bull males weighing up to 11.5 tons. Females are much smaller, averaging 3.3 tons. Elephants also have the longest pregnancy of any mammal, carrying their babies in the womb for almost twenty-two months. Cows give birth to one calf every two to four years. Females and their young live in herds of six to seventy members. Several family units may join together to form a "clan" consisting of up to several hundred members led by a female matriarch (the eldest female). Adolescent males leave the herd to live alone or in smaller bachelor herds. They eat up to five hundred pounds of vegetation a day.

Nubian ibex live in the desert mountains of the Middle East and northern Africa. They are incredibly agile, swiftly running up and down steep cliffs where few other animals can live. The females live in herds of up to twenty members and give birth to one kid, occasionally twins. Males live in smaller bands of up to eight members. They join the females during breeding season, when the males clash with each other by charging and ramming their meter-long horns together. Ibex eat mainly grasses and leaves.

Polar bears are born in land dens, but they spend most of their time on the sea ice within the Arctic Circle. A thick layer of body fat and an outer layer of hollow fur insulates them from freezing temperatures. Polar bears are strong swimmers and hunt mainly seals. They will live on fat reserves when food is scarce. Mothers usually give birth to two cubs at a time, although they can range between one and four. Cubs are born weighing less than two pounds, but they grow to become the largest carnivorous land mammals on earth.

Red-necked wallabies are common to parts of eastern Australia and Tasmania. They are marsupials, giving birth to a single embryonic joey. Tiny, blind, and hairless, the joey crawls into his mother's pouch immediately after birth to grow for another 280 days. Unlike many animals, mother wallabies will adopt and care for another motherless joey. Wallabies are usually solitary, but they will gather when there is an abundance of food and water. They eat at night, foraging on grasses and leaved plants, and sleep during the day.

Zanzibar red colobus monkeys are mainly arboreal (living in trees) within scattered forests of the Zanzibar archipelago. They live in social groups of forty to fifty individuals, with members often playing with and grooming each other. Mothers have one or two newborns each year, sharing parental care with multiple females in the group. These monkeys eat leaves, many of which contain toxic compounds. To process these, they have an elongated digestive tract, an adaptation that gives them a pronounced potbelly. They also eat charcoal, which helps absorb the toxins.

Golden jackals live in bonded breeding pairs. Mothers give birth to one to nine, usually two to four, pups within a den. During the first few weeks, she never leaves her pups, while her mate and yearlings from the previous year help by bringing food. Jackals are highly verbal, calling to each member of the pack through yelps and howls. They feed on rodents, young gazelle, hares, birds, reptiles, amphibians, fish, insects, eggs, fruit, and carrion. This canine is native to northern Africa, Southeast Europe, the Middle East, and southern Asia.

Mountain gorillas live in close-knit family groups, called "troops," which are led by a dominant male, called a silverback (for the silvery gray hair on his back). The females have only one baby every four to five years. Newborns are tiny and helpless, clinging to their mother's fur for the first several months. When they are older, much of their day is spent chasing one another, wrestling, and swinging from branches. Mountain gorillas eat mainly leaves. They are critically endangered due to habitat loss and illegal hunting. Only two wild populations remain, in the dense mountain rain forest of Central Africa.

Mustangs, also called feral horses, are free-roaming horses that live in the grasslands of the American West. They descended from horses brought to the Americas by the Spanish and live in herds consisting of one stallion, about eight females, and their young. Each herd is led by a dominant female and male. In dangerous situations, the head mare will lead her herd to safety, while the stallion stays and fights. Females give birth to one foal each year. They mostly eat grass and brush.

Brown bears are a threatened species but can still be found in many different habitats of western United States, Canada, and northern Eurasia. The cubs (usually twins) are born tiny (less than a pound), within a winter den, but grow up to two hundred pounds in their first year. They remain with their mother for the first two to three years, during which she teaches them how to find food, such as roots, grasses, fruit, fish, cashed seeds, and carrion. They occasionally hunt.

Belding's ground squirrel is a relatively small species of ground squirrel living in mountain alpine and subalpine meadows of the western United States. They eat mostly seeds, nuts, plant material, and mushrooms, but also insects and carrion. Females do all the parenting as males disperse directly after mating. Related females may share food and burrows. They give birth to a litter of three to eight pups each year. The pups spend twenty-five to twenty-eight days belowground before emerging.

North American river otters are renowned for their sense of play. Even through adulthood, they wrestle, slide, and chase. In early spring, expectant mothers find an abandoned den, made previously by a beaver or other animal, in which to give birth to her litter of one to six pups. Otters are semiaquatic, living on both land and water. They eat mostly fish but also consume amphibians, freshwater clams, mussels, snails, small turtles, and crayfish. They are widespread along waterways throughout much of North America.

Common ravens occur over most of the Northern Hemisphere in nearly any habitat. Part of their success is due to their adaptable diet; they feed on carrion, insects, grains, berries, fruit, and small animals. They build their nests on cliffs, in trees, and on tall man-made structures. Juvenile ravens are among the most playful of bird species. They have been observed to slide down snowbanks, drop sticks midair and dive to catch them, and play "Catch Me If You Can" with wolves, otters, and dogs.

Coyotes are a canine native to North America. They live in packs, consisting of a family unit or unrelated individuals. Pregnant females line a den with grasses and fur pulled from her belly and then give birth to an average litter of six pups. Her mate, and sometimes her adult sisters, will bring food back while she remains with the pups. Unlike wolf pups, coyote pups begin to seriously fight first before engaging in play behavior. By the age of five weeks, pups have established dominance hierarchies and are by then more likely to play than fight. They eat a varied diet of animal meat and occasionally fruits and vegetables.

The **common bottlenose dolphin** has a larger brain than a human's and is highly intelligent. They live in groups, called "pods," and communicate with each other by a complex system of squeaks and whistles. They work as a team to harvest schools of fish, eels, squid, and shrimp. Dolphins search for prey primarily using echolocation, by emitting up to one thousand clicking sounds per second then listening for the return echoes to determine the location of prey. They are sleek swimmers, reaching speeds of eighteen miles per hour. This species is found in the tropical oceans and other warm water worldwide.

Glossary

aggression—Behavior intended to increase an animal's dominance or rank

blowhole—The nostril of a dolphin (or whale) on the top of its head

breed—To produce offspring

canine—An animal in the dog family

carrion—The decaying flesh of dead animals

coordination—The ability to smoothly and efficiently use different parts of the body together

dominance—The most powerful position or rank in a group

foal—A young horse

forage—To search for food

gamboling—The swinging movement of an animal's head and shoulders from side to side

joey—A young wallaby or other marsupial

kid—A young goat

kit—The young of certain animals, such as jackals or foxes

litter—The group of animals born to one female at one time

pack—A group of animals operating together

predator—An animal that kills and eats other animals (the prey)

prey—An animal that is killed and eaten by another animal (the predator)

retracted—Drawn back or in (such as an animal's claws, to avoid scratching)

sibling—A brother or sister having one or more parents in common

snout—The projecting nose and mouth of an animal

stalk—To quietly and patiently hunt an animal

vortices—Whirlpools of swirling fluid and bubbles

yearling—An animal one year old or in its second year

Sources

Bateson, Patrick and Paul Martin. *Play, Playfulness, Creativity and Innovation*. Cambridge, UK: Cambridge University Press, 2013.

Burghardt, Gordon M. *The Genesis of Animal Play: Testing the Limits*. Cambridge, MA: The MIT Press, 2006.

Elbroch, Mark, and Kurt Rinehart. *Peterson Reference Guide to the Behavior of North American Mammals*. Boston: Houghton Mifflin Harcourt, 2011.

Estes, Richard Despard. *The Behavior Guide to African Mammals: Including Hoofed Mammals, Carnivores, Primates*. Illustrated by Daniel Otte. Berkeley, CA: The University of California Press, 2012.

Fagen, Robert. *Animal Play Behavior*. New York: Oxford University Press, 1981.

Macdonald, David W., ed. *The Princeton Encyclopedia of Mammals*. Princeton, NJ: Princeton University Press, 2009.

National Geographic Society. *National Geographic Book of Mammals*. Washington, DC: National Geographic, 1998.

Parker, Steve. *DK Eyewitness Books: Mammal*. New York: DK, 2004.

Power, Thomas G. *Play and Exploration in Children and Animals*. New York; Hove: Psychology Press, 2013.

Reid, Fiona A. *A Field Guide to Mammals of North America, North of Mexico*. Boston: Houghton Mifflin, 2006.

Good Websites for More Information

Animal Diversity Web: animaldiversity.org
National Geographic: animals.nationalgeographic.com/animals
National Wildlife Federation: nwf.org/Wildlife.aspx
Ranger Rick: rangerrick.org
Smithsonian's National Zoo: nationalzoo.si.edu/animals
World Wildlife Fund: worldwildlife.org/species